ANSEL
ADAMS

ANSEL ADAMS

BARRY PRITZKER

BISON GROUP

First published in the UK in 1991
Brompton Books
a division of the Bison Group
Kimbolton House
117A Fulham Road,
London, SW3 6RL

ISBN 0-86124-686-1

Printed in Hong Kong

Reprinted 1993

Most of the photographs in this collection were reproduced from negatives of original Ansel Adams prints preserved by the National Archives rather than from original negatives.

This book has not been authorized by and has no connection with Ansel Adams and the Ansel Adams Publishing Rights Trust.

Acknowledgments
The author and publisher would like to thank the following people who helped in the preparation of this book: Design 23; Susan Bernstein, the Editor; and Rita Longabucco, the picture editor.

Page 1:
"Grand Canyon National Park,"
Grand Canyon National Park, Arizona.

Page 2:
"Yellowstone Falls,"
Yellowstone National Park, Wyoming.

Page 5:
"Court of the Patriarchs,"
Zion National Park, Utah.

Contents

INTRODUCTION

One always wonders at the role of chance in human events. In the spring of 1916 fourteen-year-old Ansel Adams, never a healthy boy, took to his bed again. This time the problem was only a cold; young Ansel was pleased that the illness was not serious enough to prevent him from accompanying his family on a vacation that was scheduled for early that summer, though the destination was as yet undecided.

To help him pass the time in bed his Aunt Mary gave him a book entitled *In the Heart of the Sierras*, by J. M. Hutchings. Ansel fell in love with the descriptions and illustrations of those mountains and convinced his family to head east to Yosemite for their vacation. He was to return at least once every year of his life. Although as a young man he studied music and seriously considered a career as a concert pianist, many years later Ansel Adams, one of the world's best-loved and most successful photographers, said of first time he saw the Sierra, "I knew my destiny when I first experienced Yosemite."

Ansel Adams received his first camera from his father, a Kodak #1 Box Brownie, in 1916. At the time photography was barely 100 years old, and taken seriously as an art form by only a handful of people. In a lifetime devoted to expressing his own creativity and to establishing firmly the validity of artistic photography, Adams personally made more than 40,000 negatives, signed 10,000 fine prints, exhibited his work in more than 500 exhibitions, and sold over one million copies of his books. Through his photographs he made millions of people aware not only of the natural beauty of the western United States but also, as an ardent and outspoken conservationist, of the need to preserve and protect that beauty for the pleasure of future generations.

Ansel Easton Adams was born on February 20, 1902, in what was then a natural and somewhat wild part of San Francisco. Out on the dunes west of the city, the family home commanded a magnificent view of the Golden Gate, the rolling hills of Marin County, and the Pacific Ocean. Growing up on the central California coast taught him to appreciate the light and mystery of profound natural beauty. His father, Charles Hitchcock Adams, encouraged that view, and added to it a healthy dose of the Puritan work ethic and sense of duty.

The elder Adams had an enormous influence on his son. The Adams family originally hailed from New England. Charles Adams, though born in California, had a strong belief in the Emersonian ideal of self reliance and the primacy of the human spirit. He conveyed this to Ansel in many ways: in his intense relationship with nature; in his example of strict personal honesty and integrity, despite a continuing series of financial disasters; and in his utter confidence in the creative spirit of his son. Charles, or Carlie, as he was known, was not all work,

however. Whenever possible he liked to indulge in his favorite hobby, photography. Throughout his life Ansel maintained an enduring admiration and respect for his father.

Ansel's relationship to his mother, Olive, was not as close. Her family, the Brays, came from Baltimore, although they moved to Carson City, Nevada, in the mid-nineteenth century. Shortly after her marriage to Carlie, Olive began to suffer from a progressively debilitating depression. Ansel never quite understood the reasons for his mother's condition. For years he knew only that his parents were unhappy and that his mother's father and sister, who lived with the Adamses until their deaths, were a financial burden for his father.

Ansel Adams did not easily adapt to the discipline of traditional schooling as a child. Why sit in school when you could be outdoors? He was probably hyperactive, and certainly was physically ill and emotionally distraught with frustrating regularity. By the age of thirteen it was clear to all that Ansel was not succeeding in school. Despite his belief in education, Carlie Adams was enough of an individualist and a nonconformist to appreciate the uniqueness of his son. He proposed a radical plan: for the coming year, Ansel would not attend classes at school. Instead, he would travel every day to the Panama-Pacific International Exposition, held in San Francisco that year to celebrate the opening of the Panama Canal, to learn what he could about the world.

This exposition was Adams's classroom for a year. Sometimes his father would accompany him, and together they would explore the exhibits. The exposition also offered the opportunity to study a wide selection of contemporary painting, including works by Cézanne, Gauguin, and Monet. At a show a year later, Adams was exposed to the latest ideas in art — the cubist works of Picasso and Braque.

The stimulation and informal structure of the exposition coupled with a series of private tutors, succeeded where more traditional means had failed: Adams finally graduated from the eighth grade and received his grammar school diploma in 1917. About that time, he began to take an interest in an old piano that had sat for years in a corner of the living room. He soon taught himself to play the instrument, while Carlie, pleased by the talent and initiative displayed by his son, arranged for formal lessons. He found piano teachers who maintained the highest standards and insisted that their students do the same. Eventually Adams became an accomplished pianist. His musical studies helped him to structure his life by teaching him both discipline and the value of striving to achieve his best.

After graduation, Adams took a job in San Francisco with a photo-finishing company. Two years later, bored with the repetitive nature of the work and very much under the influence

Above:
Eadweard J. Muybridge's 1872 photograph
"Falls of the Yosemite from Glacier Rock."
Adams said, "I knew my destiny when
I first experienced Yosemite."

of his trips to the mountains, he began a stint as custodian at the headquarters of the Sierra Club at Yosemite National Park. In 1920 Adams undertook his first true wilderness trip. Together with "Uncle" Frank Holman, a family friend and avid mountaineer he scaled the breathtaking heights, explored the serene valleys, and swam in the pure lakes of Yosemite. Adams carried his camera equipment all over the park and took many fine pictures.

Although he was still seriously studying the piano, photography began to take an ever greater hold on his imagination. He preferred Yosemite in winter because of the greater opportunities for black-and-white contrasts. He hiked for pleasure and also to study different approaches to mountain photography. He already had definite ideas concerning the way in which to compose a photograph and the proper lighting needed to achieve a certain effect. On occasion he would wait someplace for hours, or perhaps most of a day, for the right light in which to finally click the shutter. His aim never was to make a mere record of a subject or scene, but rather to create an artistic expression.

In the early days Adams preferred an impressionistic style of photography. At first he printed "soft-focus" negatives, reflecting the prevailing idea that photographs had to look like charcoal drawings to be "artistic." However, he soon aban-

doned that process in favor of a more direct style that was for him optically more accurate, vivid, and emotionally satisfying. Although the water necessary for the printing process was hard to come by at the Sierra Club's LeConte Memorial Lodge (it had to be brought in big buckets), Adams would never think of letting someone else print his negatives. Carefully controlled, top-quality printing, as well as a focus on the unspoiled natural world, was from the beginning a trademark of the photographs of Ansel Adams.

Many of Adams's central ideas concerning the nature of photography were formed during this period of his life. Adams had no time for people who spoke of photographs as "objective" creations, as opposed to paintings, which were thought of as more interpretive or "artistic." He insisted that, far from being objective, a photographer has to carefully consider many crucial variables before taking a picture: composition of a photograph, correct lens to create the right visual effect, film, filter, and light. In the hands of skilled artists all these elements combine to record "a private glimpse of some ideal reality."

In fact, one mark of Adams's genius as a photographer was his ability to "visualize" the outcome of a picture before it was actually made. "Visualization," an important Adams term, involves "the intuitive search for meaning, shape, form, texture, and the projection of the image-format on the subject." This

would not have been possible without both his particular brand of creative inspiration and his excellent command of the many technical aspects of the photographic process.

Throughout the early 1920s Adams led mountaineering trips for the Sierra Club. Faculty members from Stanford or the University of California at Berkeley often enrolled in these expeditions; they provided good company for their unschooled but intellectually curious guide. The Sierra Club soon recognized the quality of Adams's photographs, and began publishing them along with articles related to his hikes in *The Sierra Club Bulletin*.

During his stays at Yosemite he also found the time to keep up with his music studies. His friend Harry Best, of Best's Photographic Studio, allowed Ansel to practice on his piano. It was at Best's Studio that he met Virginia Best, the daughter of the proprietor and Adams's future wife.

It was also during this period that Adams made the acquaintance of Albert Bender, a wealthy and influential patron of the arts in the Bay area. Bender took a strong interest in Adams, introducing him to the local art scene and eventually commissioning several portfolios. Casting about for the theme of one book, Adams drew upon his love of the American Southwest, having become enamored of that region during a trip there with Bender in 1927. The resulting portfolio of the ancient Taos Pueblo was published in 1930, in an edition of 100 books. At the time each sold for $75; by the mid-1980s Adams's *Taos Pueblo* was selling for around $12,000.

In Taos, Adams stayed at the ranch of arts hostess Mabel Dodge Luhan. There he met Georgia O'Keeffe, Paul Strand, and a number of other artists. Although he would remain friendly with O'Keeffe, and her husband Alfred Stieglitz, for many years, it was Strand who was to change his life. One afternoon he invited Adams to look at his negatives. Adams was bowled over: he had never seen such subtlety of light, such perfect composition – simple, yet so powerful. For the first time Adams clearly understood the potential of photography as an expressive art. By the time he returned to San Francisco he no longer wondered whether his future lay in music or photography. He had made his decision.

Fortunately his wife Virginia agreed with his career choice. They had married in 1928. In 1930, following his decision to concentrate on photography, he built a house in San Francisco and began soliciting commercial assignments. These he viewed as a bargain with the devil: he needed commercial work to make a living, but he always made a distinction between commercial ("without") and creative ("within") photography, saving his best work for the latter. For instance, he consented to shoot color film for commercial assignments, but rarely used it for his artistic endeavors, believing that only with black-and-white film could he sufficiently control the photographic process and convey a profound emotional depth. His commercial clients eventually included such companies as Pacific Gas and Electric, American Telegraph and Telephone, American Trust, Eastman-Kodak, Hills Brothers Coffee, and his most im-

Opposite: Above all others it was Paul Strand who deeply influenced Adams. Here is Strand's "The White Fence, Port Kent, 1916."

Above: Alfred Stieglitz gave Adams confidence that he could express himself through photography. Here is Stieglitz's "Spring Showers."

Above: Georgia O'Keeffe at an exhibition of her work in 1931. Adams's meeting with her in 1927 was the start of a lifelong friendship.

Above: Adams wrote photographic
reviews about French photographer
Eugene Atget. Here is Atget's "Boulevard
de Strasbourg, Corsets, 1912."

portant client for many years, The Yosemite Park and Curry Company.

Within a year he was writing photography reviews for the magazine, *The Fortnightly*. His subjects included Eugene Atget and Edward Weston, the latter of whom eventually became his close friend. By 1932 Virginia was pregnant with their first child, Michael. In 1934 Adams and several other influential Bay area photographers, including Imogen Cunningham and Edward Weston, decided to create a formal association with the goal of advancing photography as an art form. Known as Group f/64 – 64 being the smallest aperture setting on a camera, allowing the greatest depth of field and hence the maximum sharpness throughout a photograph – these artists were dedicated to what they called "pure" photography.

They defined pure photography as "possessing no qualities of technique, composition, or idea, derivative of any other art form. . . . [they believed that] photography, as an art form, must develop along lines defined by the actualities and limitations of the photographic medium. . ." Most of these artists used a view camera with an 8 × 10 negative, as well as a lens which provided the most extreme optical sharpness. They insisted on using glossy paper on which to print their negatives. In short, they popularized the idea that a photograph should look like photograph, not like an imitation of another art form.

While Group f/64 helped to create a mini-renaissance of photography in the San Francisco Bay area, the center of art photography in America was New York City; specifically, a gallery called An American Place, owned by the man generally acknowledged to be the master of the medium, Alfred Stieglitz. In 1933 Adams traveled east to meet the great man. Adams knew his own work was good, but hardly dared hope that Stieglitz would agree. To his delight, Stieglitz liked his work, and even offered to arrange a show at the Place. (Adams did have his New York one-man exhibition debut during that trip, but it

Left: "The Steerage, 1907," by Alfred Stieglitz.

Opposite: Imogen Cunningham along with Adams and other photographers formed Group f/64. Here is Cunningham's "Magnolia Blossom, 1925."

was at a gallery called Delphic Studios. He had to wait three years to show his work at the Place.)

Adams was elated. To him, recognition by Stieglitz meant that he now belonged to a worldwide tradition in photography, including not only early Americans like Timothy O'Sullivan and William Henry Jackson, but also such masters as Eugene Atget and even Stieglitz himself. Adams later said that Stieglitz did not so much influence him as he gave him the confidence that he could express himself through photography. His credo, "Art is the affirmation of life," he learned from Stieglitz. When he returned home, still excited about his meeting with Stieglitz, Adams opened the short-lived Ansel Adams Gallery in San Francisco.

The year 1936 was a busy one for Ansel Adams. His second child, Anne, had been born just the year before. As a member of the Board of Directors of the Sierra Club (he had been elected in 1934) he traveled to Washington, D.C., to lobby for the creation of a new national park at Kings River Canyon, California. There he used photographs as a lobbying tool, noting that photographs of the Sierra by Carleton Watkins influenced the decision to create a state park at Yosemite Valley

in 1864, and W.H. Jackson's photographs of Yellowstone played a major role in the establishment of our first national park in 1872. While in Washington he also met Secretary of the Interior Harold Ickes, a man who would be instrumental in obtaining for Adams a major commission – later known as the Mural Project – to photograph sites under the jurisdiction of the Interior Department. Adams also had his exhibition at An American Place in 1936. Meanwhile, Virginia's father had died. She and Ansel prepared to move the family to Yosemite and assume control of Best's Studio.

Thanks largely to the influence of Adams and the other members of Group f/64, Stieglitz, and such art historians as Beaumont and Nancy Newhall, with whom Adams had recently become friendly, photography was rapidly gaining acceptance as a fine art. Perhaps the ultimate evidence of this was the decision by the Trustees of New York's Museum of Modern Art to create a Department of Photography within the museum. Newhall was the curator of the new department, and David McAlpin, a businessman, arts patron, and key sponsor of the project, was the chairman of the Photography Committee. In 1940 Adams agreed to a request by Newhall and McAlpin to

13

come to New York for six months as a special advisor to help launch the new department. The first exhibit of the Department of Photography at the Museum of Modern Art opened on December 31, 1940. Entitled "Sixty Photographs," it featured a survey of photography from the 1840s calotypes of David Octavius Hill and Robert Adamson to contemporary photographs by artists such as Adams, Weston, and Stieglitz.

As exciting as the MoMA project was, Adams did not enjoy his stay in New York (once he admitted that he had a hard time appreciating America east of Denver!). Early in 1940 Adams began teaching at the Art Center School in Los Angeles. It was his first serious teaching experience, and one which he thoroughly enjoyed. Teaching came easily to Adams, in part, no doubt, because he shared his father's belief in the value of passing down knowledge to others for the edification of future generations.

In an effort to systematize his teaching method, Adams developed one of his most fundamental technical innovations. The Zone System is a codification of what might be called the Adams System for creating a technically proficient photograph. It divides the range of light into eleven tones, or zones, from total black (zone zero) to pure white (zone ten). With this system the photographer can determine and then create specific tones in a final print based on an assessment of the contrast range of a subject. He always stressed, however, that the Zone

Opposite top: "Yellowstone Lake, Mt Sheridan," taken by Adams while working on the Mural Project.

Opposite bottom: Adams used his photographs of Kings River Canyon, California, as a lobbying tool to try to create a new national park. Here is Adams's "Mt. Winchell."

Right: Adams admired the work of Dorothea Lange. Here is Lange's "Migrant Worker, Nipomo, California, 1936."

System was a strictly technical tool, and merely a complement to, not a substitution for, individual creative vision.

Though a pacifist at heart, Adams did try to enlist in the fight against what he called "the hideous Hitler regime," but was rejected since he was a married forty-year-old with dependents. Still, he undertook a number of civilian assignments, including escorting American troops around Yosemite Valley, teaching practical photography at Fort Ord, and printing some top-secret negatives of Japanese military installations. In the fall of 1943 he visited the Manzanar War Relocation Camp in Owens Valley, three hundred miles north of Los Angeles, and landed an assignment from the director of the camp to photograph its people and the life they made there. Adams was impressed both with the courage and fortitude of the loyal Japanese-American citizens imprisoned at Manzanar and with the natural beauty he found in and around Owens Valley. His book of photographs

from the project, *Born Free and Equal*, was published in 1944.

Adams also used his growing celebrity as a photographer in the service of the war effort. He knew, of course, that millions of people saw his work, either in exhibitions or in one of his many books. In the early 1940s his photographs begin to reflect a particularly optimistic and even heroic quality. To Americans burdened with war, he showed an expansive country, full of hope and promise. Interestingly, Adams objected to most documentary photography. He admired the images of Dorothea Lange – best known for her work in the thirties for the Farm Security Administration – because he felt they conveyed a broad range of human emotions. In general, however, the man who was fond of saying that there was as much social significance in a rock as in a breadline disliked being told what was important and what wasn't. Ever a champion of the individual, Adams saw too much of the group in most documentary work.

He especially disliked what he considered the negativity in documentary photography. Where, he often wondered, were the positive aspects of America – the "ordinary, healthy, reasonably smart, reasonably aware, reasonably successful people?" Where was the "Whitmanesque" aspect of America – joyous, celebratory, wildly optimistic? Adams disliked Edward Steichen for a number of reasons, many having to do with conflicting personalities, but primarily because he believed that Steichen's photographs reflected a fear of the beautiful. He condemned the degeneration of photography in the hands of Steichen, and many others, into "mere pictorialism" – or worse, into propaganda.

During the early years of the war Adams had a unique opportunity, as the official photographer of the Mural Project, to travel throughout the American West courtesy of the U.S. government, taking pictures of Indian reservations and many of the national parks and other facilities under the control of the Interior Department in that region. His compensation was the maximum allowed at the time for consultants, $22.22 per day, plus costs including car expenses at 4 cents per mile. The award of two Guggenheim Fellowships, one in 1946 and another in 1948, allowed Adams to pursue another dream – an extended photography trip to the territory of Alaska.

There he found the natural scenery as awesome as he had hoped. When the weather was good he covered many miles in a variety of very basic airplanes, seeing a good deal of the exquisite Alaskan landscape. Unfortunately the weather was often poor; when it was, Adams contented himself with shooting close-ups and intimate studies of nature. He also used his time off to reflect on the tension between wilderness and civilization. He had always found meaning and inspiration in wilderness, but in Alaska for the first time he felt the full force of vast, natural space. It seemed to Adams that, as magnificent as he found the national parks in the continental U.S., including his beloved Yosemite, they all were relatively confined and threatened with over-development. As he watched the rain pour down at Glacier Bay, he realized that, for both body and soul, human beings need the existence of large areas of unspoiled wilderness on our planet. He determined from then on to devote whatever resources he could to save our environment, especially wilderness, from further destruction.

One result of his prodigious work with the camera was the accelerated pace of his publications. The first two of four volumes in his "Basic Photo Series," *Camera and Lens* and *The Negative*, were published in 1948, with the third and fourth volumes coming out in the early 1950s. In fact, during the first half of the 1950s Adams published no fewer than eight books; helped to found, with Minor White and others, the new photography journal *Aperture*; and teamed up with Dorothea Lange to do a photo-essay in *Life* on the Mormons in Utah. He also struck up a deep friendship with Dr. Edwin Land, innovator of the instant photographic process. Their friendship was based on profound mutual respect and on a shared interest in the technical aspects of photography. In 1949 Adams became a consultant for the newly founded Polaroid Corporation.

His passion for teaching, first discovered in 1940, flourished anew in 1955 with the genesis of the Ansel Adams Workshops. Adams took pleasure in helping students to discover their own creativity through photography. The workshops were held at Yosemite every year from 1955 until 1981, when advancing age forced him to move the workshops to his home in Carmel. His main teaching tools consisted of the Zone System and his concept of visualizing of a photograph. What is seen, he would ask his students? How is it seen, and how is it executed? He often advised his students to try to "read" a photograph; that is, to try to imagine what the reality might have been with only a photograph as evidence.

By the late 1950s Ansel and Virginia had lived at Yosemite for twenty years, and had been visiting there for more than forty. Unabashed partisans of that wonderful park, they had been bothered for some time that the souvenirs available to tourists were of poor quality, or tasteless, or both. In order to improve the image of the park he loved, and to help leave tourists with more dignified and appropriate memories, Ansel began to produce a series of "Yosemite Special Edition Prints." He did not print the negatives himself, but true to his philosophy of adhering to the highest standards, they were printed by his assistants to meet his special requirements. Available only at Best's Studio, Adams sold thousands of these beautiful, inexpensive 8 × 10-inch prints over the years.

To say that Adams was slowing down as he reached his sixties is only to acknowledge that his schedule began to approximate that of the average forty-year-old. Feeling the need for a change, he and Virginia left Yosemite in 1962 to return to the ocean, this time to a magnificent home built for them in Carmel Highlands, California. Yet this was not a retirement home for Ansel: he was still taking pictures (though he took few significant ones after the move west), still putting in long hours in his darkroom, still publishing books and arranging for exhibitions. If this wasn't enough to keep him busy, he often had time, after a day of hard work, to entertain friends and visitors, even to look at a portfolio an eager student might bring to show him.

He also had the time, and the energy, to begin a major new photographic association. Ever since his friend Edward Weston died in 1958, Adams had carried on the family friendship with Weston's sons, Cole and Brett. In 1966, with the encouragement of Cole Weston, Adams got some like-minded people together and formed The Friends of Photography, a non-profit organization dedicated to the advancement of creative photography. From the beginning Adams was the president of the board of trustees, and although many people helped to shape the direction and tone of the group, there could be no doubt that Ansel Adams was its moving force and chief inspiration.

Especially under the able leadership of James Alinder, The Friends eventually grew into the largest international group of its kind, with a sound financial base, a membership, as of the mid-1980s, of more than 12,000, an educational program

Above: Ansel Adams in 1966.

Right: Edward Weston was a Group f/64 member and Adams's friend. Here is Weston's "Two Shells, 1927."

featuring the Ansel Adams Workshops, and an impressive series of exhibitions. One of the more ambitious projects of The Friends was the production in Shanghai of a major Ansel Adams exhibition. Five thousand people waited each day to view the great American photographer's work. After the Shanghai show the exhibition was installed in the Beijing Museum of Art. Adams took pride in his ability to act as a cultural emissary during a time of tension between the United States and China.

In fact, his love of and dedication to The Friends of Photography was such that he and Virginia decided to leave their home and studio to the group after their deaths. He hoped that this final act of "passing down" would help The Friends to succeed as a thriving organization. The bequest of his home was only one of the gifts Adams made in his later years. In 1977, to honor his dear friends, Adams established the Beaumont and Nancy Newhall Curatorial Fellowship in Photography at the

Museum of Modern Art. In 1975 he helped to establish the Center for Creative Photography at the University of Arizona in Tucson, now his archive and the repository of his negatives.

In addition to teaching and working with The Friends, Adams kept up a busy travel schedule, personally accepting many of the awards that came his way, and continued to work on his publications and other projects. In 1966 he was elected a fellow of the American Academy of Arts and Sciences. In 1974 Adams traveled to Europe for the first time, where he taught at the Arles (France) photography festival. In 1976 he journeyed to London to attend the opening of his major exhibition at the Victoria and Albert Museum. In 1974, and again in 1979, the Museum of Modern Art mounted a major retrospective of his work. Although he had resigned from the Sierra Club's board of directors in 1971 – as a result of a political dispute with its leadership, after 37 years of service – he was elected an honorary vice-president of that group in 1978. In 1980 the Wilderness Society established the Ansel Adams Conservation Award naming its namesake as the first recipient.

Adams's falling out with the Sierra Club was a sign not only of his "militant optimism" (he despised what he perceived as both the negativity of the president, David Browser, and the unrealistically hardline stance of the club in their fight with Pacific Gas and Electric (PG&E) over the siting of the Diablo Canyon nuclear power plant); it also reflected his growing political activism. As an activist he did not shun controversy. He certainly saw himself as a committed conservationist, but he also, characteristically, believed in acknowledging what he considered certain social and economic realities.

Above: Ansel Adams at work.

Left: Ansel Adams holds the Hasselblad Award presented to him by Sweden's King Carl XVI Gustaf and Queen Silvia in 1981.

Opposite: Ansel Adams at the Academy of Natural Sciences of Philadelphia. He was awarded the Academy's 1981 Gold Medal for distinction in natural history art.

For example, PG&E originally wanted to site their nuclear power plant on the Nipomo Dunes, a region which Adams and the rest of the Sierra Club held to be of incalculable ecological significance. The club, divided on the issue but under the influence of Adams, prevailed upon PG&E to move the site to Diablo Canyon (this was before the club knew about the earthquake fault). Adams said later that as a natural area, "the Dunes are far more important than Diablo Canyon," a position for which he was soundly criticized by some of his environmentalist friends. In another instance, Adams, chided for working on a commercial for Datsun automobiles, maintained that since cars are here to stay, the public may as well be encouraged to drive fuel-efficient ones.

Ansel Adams personally lobbied Presidents Ford, Carter, and Reagan to conserve and respect the environment. He liked the Fords, and applauded the conservation efforts of President Carter. When asked to photograph Jimmy and Rosalynn Carter for the official presidential portrait (the first time a photograph was used instead of a painting) Adams humbly accepted. In 1979 President Carter awarded him the Presidential Medal of Freedom, America's highest civilian honor. Even Adams, however, try as he might to be positive, could not see anything hopeful in a Ronald Reagan presidency. He believed that James Watt's appointment as Secretary of the Interior was the single most disastrous environmental decision of the century, and regarded Reagan himself as hostile to the environment.

The awards and tributes continued through his eighth decade and into his ninth. In 1981 the Swedes awarded him the Hasselblad Medal, named after the man who created one of his favorite cameras, and in the same year he was awarded an honorary Doctor of Fine Arts degree from Harvard University (his first such award came from the University of California at Berkeley in 1961). In 1982 he received the French Legion of Merit. For his eightieth birthday, the pianist Vladimir Ashkenazy played for him at his home. However, even decades of mountain climbing couldn't make his heart last forever. In 1979 he underwent successful triple bypass surgery, and in 1982 a pacemaker was installed. Ansel Adams died of heart failure on April 22, 1984.

As is often the case with great figures, Adams's impact upon the world has continued, and will endure, long after his death. Thanks to the efforts of Senators Pete Wilson and Alan Cranston, the California legislature passed the California Wilderness Bill, designating more than 100,000 acres of the Sierra as the Ansel Adams Wilderness Area. On the first anniversary of his death, an 11,760-foot peak at the head of the Lyell Fork of the Merced River, in Yosemite National Park, was officially named Mt. Ansel Adams. Several of his books have been published posthumously, including his autobiography, with Mary Street Alinder, and major exhibitions of his works have been held in San Francisco and Washington.

But it is his art, of course, that surely is his gift to the world. Adams once said that he never intentionally made a creative photograph that related directly to an environmental issue; that he never knew in advance precisely what he would photograph because he could not command the creative impulse on demand. Art, for Adams, was "the exact opposite of the pictorial, human-interest . . . and popular. . . It relates to the depth of experience and perception." Although he believed that photographs of nature were not necessarily artistic, it was nature that was his never-ending inspiration, and all that he could find to compare with the splendor of the natural universe was the creative work of the human spirit. Ansel Adams undoubtedly counted himself among "the relatively few authentic creators of [his] time," who possessed, in truth, "a resonance with eternity."

CANYONS AND CAVERNS

Ansel Adams traveled to Grand Canyon and Carlsbad Caverns National Parks as part of the Mural Project, a government plan to photograph national parks and monuments, Indian reservations, and other sites under the control of the Department of the Interior. The project, as conceived by Secretary of the Interior Harold Ickes in the mid-1930s, was to result either in large paintings or in photographic images suitable for enlargement to mural size, which would then be hung in the offices of the Interior Department building located in Washington, D.C.

Adams knew a great opportunity when he saw it: throughout the late 1930s and into the 1940s he courted Ickes with the express purpose of winning the Mural Project commission. By October 1941, he had succeeded in his quest and was out on the road with his eight-year-old son, Michael, and one of his best friends, Cedric Wright. They spent much of that fall driving around the back roads of New Mexico, taking pictures and taking in the subtle but powerful mystery of the desert. In the spring of 1942 Adams continued his travels, this time in the northern Rockies, and by train.

Unfortunately, due to the pressure of World War II, the Mural Project was abandoned on July 1, 1942. Harold Ickes departed from the Interior Department in 1946. The project was not revived after the war, and the murals were never made. However, this did not stop Adams from his work in the national parks. He applied for, and received, a Guggenheim Fellowship in 1946, which was renewed in 1948. By 1950 Adams succeeded in making extensive photographs of many of America's national parks and monuments, even traveling to the land of the greatest wilderness in the United States, Alaska.

From his first visit to the Southwest, in 1927, Adams had been captivated by the diversity of geographic forms, the ever-changing light and almost primordial force of the desert. Like high mountain regions, the desert appears rugged but is in truth extremely fragile. The lack of trees contributes to the feeling of permanence; there is nothing to hide the huge vistas of sand and rock. Water, as basic to human life as air, is largely absent in the rural Southwest. Sheep trails and arroyos, following the land's eternal contours, are gentle on the eye, while paved roads, auto camps, and billboards break up the land and assault the senses.

One such affront, signs for Whites' Cabins, greeted Adams on his way to photograph Carlsbad Caverns. Several days before encountering the endless billboards, Ansel and Michael were heading back to Santa Fe after an unsuccessful day with the camera, approaching the village of Hernandez near sunset. At once the visualization came to Adams; he jumped out of the car, set up the camera, and soon had perhaps his most famous negative, "Moonrise, Hernandez, New Mexico." Later, after passing through White Sands National Monument, Adams and crew pulled up at Whites' and prepared to view the caverns.

They proved a challenging subject, owing largely to the dim electric light which illuminated the limestone formations. Adams feared that the lighting was arranged merely to provide a theatrical effect, and tried to visualize a more natural, cave-like print. He took the cavern tour (experiencing "absolute darkness and the most profound silence!"), made several negatives, and resolved to return at a later date with more extension cords and lights.

His outdoor subjects were more inspiring: the awesome Grand Canyon and the magnificent Canyon de Chelly. Navigating the roads around the canyons was quite an adventure. Adams drove through – if he was lucky – giant mudholes and flooded-out washes, at one point making only sixty miles in fifteen hours, during the worst rainy season in twenty-five years. Canyon de Chelly, in the heart of Navajo country, is a visual tour de force. Although artists are often stymied by its sense of spiritual power and sheer physical scale, Ansel Adams claims to have made some of his best photographs on the rim of that canyon.

The Grand Canyon is also not easy to photograph. The top of some rock formations can tower a mile above the canyon floor, while up to eighteen miles may separate one side of the canyon from the other. The sky is often filled with haze. The effect of depth, so crucial in a photograph, is almost impossible to realize. Still, with hard work, tremendous skill, and obvious inspiration, Adams managed to achieve images of these sublime places that few before or since can match.

"Grand Canyon from North Rim, 1941,"
Grand Canyon National Park, Arizona

"Grand Canyon National Park,"
Grand Canyon National Park, Arizona

"Grand Canyon from South Rim, 1941,"
Grand Canyon National Park, Arizona

"Grand Canyon National Park,"
Grand Canyon National Park, Arizona

"Grand Canyon National Park,"
Grand Canyon National Park, Arizona

"Grand Canyon National Park,"
Grand Canyon National Park, Arizona

"Grand Canyon National Park,"
Grand Canyon National Park, Arizona

"In the Queen's Chamber,"
Carlsbad Caverns National Park, New Mexico

"Formations along the wall of the
Big Room, near the Crystal Spring Home,"
Carlsbad Caverns National Park, New Mexico

"The Giant Domes in the interior of Carlsbad Caverns,"
Carlsbad Caverns National Park, New Mexico

"Formations, along trail in the Big Room,
beyond the Temple of the Sun,"
Carlsbad Caverns National Park, New Mexico

"The Giant Dome, largest stalagmite thus far discovered,"
Carlsbad Caverns National Park, New Mexico

"Formations above Green Lake,"
Carlsbad Caverns National Park, New Mexico

"Canyon de Chelly,"
Canyon de Chelly, Arizona

MOUNTAINS AND SKIES

Ansel Adams had to wait until he was fourteen years old before he visited the mountains. Once he finally got there, he would return again and again, as though the mountains were water and he was driven by a torrid thirst that knew no end. He loved the company of people, yet just as important to him – more so, perhaps – was his solitude. For some, the steady crashing waves, the lonely cries of gulls and the eternal horizon of the ocean satisfies this need. Growing up by the Pacific Ocean, Adams might have become a son of the sea. Despite the possibilities for changing light and scrub flora at the shore, however, there are few photographs of the ocean among his works. Rocks, snow, mountains, skies, and long views into remote valleys were what interested him: Adams was primarily a man of the high country.

He cut his teeth on the high Sierra. His first trip there came during a family vacation in 1916. More than sixty years later he clearly remembered the fresh fragrance from the Digger pines, the little clouds above the granite peaks, the clear, rosy glow of his first Sierra dawn. He knew even then that the mountains had changed his life forever. In countless hikes over the years he walked alone over peaks and through valleys, encountered freak blizzards, abandoned his food – unwillingly – to bears, even survived an attack of appendicitis while thirteen miles from the nearest help. In the Sierra, as in the Rockies, Cascades, and other mountain ranges, Adams felt the magic of the cool dawn wind and stood as he said, "on the high altars, within the portals of the temple."

Of course, Adams's essential mountaineering equipment always included a camera. It is easy to overlook the fact that in order to photograph mountains, unless one always wants to shoot from the base up, one must climb them. This is easier in today's world of sophisticated equipment and lightweight alloys, but Adams had a different experience. During one expedition in the snowy high country, for instance, he hauled around a camera pack weighing forty pounds, including his "Korona view camera, several lenses, two filters, six holders containing twelve glass plates, and a heavy wooden tripod" – in addition to his camping gear! Some of Adams's most brilliant mountain photographs seem to reflect not only the majesty and splendor of the natural scene but also the artist's exuberance at attaining the perfect roost after a long and often grueling climb.

While exploring the high country, Adams also had time to develop his own personal approach to mountain photography. At age eighteen he preferred an impressionistic interpretation of his subject (a style he quickly abandoned), and was already experimenting with composition, texture, and light. He refined his method throughout the 1920s on long expeditions alone and with the Sierra Club, becoming more and more certain of the essential simplicity, yet strength of character, he wanted his photographs to convey. He was captivated by the light in the high Sierra; its unusual sharpness and clarity inspired him to visualize images with dramatic contrasts and bold textures. This is the expressive style with which he made all of his later photographs, a style clearly inspired by the drama and contrast of the mountains and high country skies.

Adams was not the first photographer-mountaineer. Professor Joseph LeConte, Francis Farquhar and William Colby of the Sierra Club, and Walter Huber were among Adams's predecessors and models. These men, some of whom were friends of John Muir, founder of the Sierra Club and naturalist par excellence, took very seriously Muir's admonition to "do something for wilderness and make the mountains glad." Adams was strongly influenced by this spirit. It moved him both to interpret his beloved mountains through his art and to try to save them through political activism.

Through nature, Adams was able to discover the meaning and truth of his own soul. He believed others could be similarly touched by nature, if they would only listen. Adams was equally creative in the mountains, the desert, at the ocean, or in a cave. Still, it was to the mountains he always returned. Perhaps it was there, above all, where he achieved a "magical union with beauty" and was inspired, again and again, to pass that feeling on. After all, he once observed, "no matter how sophisticated you may be, a large granite mountain cannot be denied."

"In Rocky Mountain National Park,"
Rocky Mountain National Park, Colorado

"Zion National Park,"
Zion National Park, Utah

"From Going-to-the-Sun Chalet,"
Glacier National Park, Montana

"Mt. Moran and Jackson Lake from Signal Hill,"
Grand Teton National Park, Wyoming

"Grand Teton,"
Grand Teton National Park, Wyoming

"Tetons from Signal Mountain,"
Grand Teton National Park, Wyoming

"Grand Teton,"

"Grand Teton,"
Grand Teton National Park, Wyoming

"Center Peak, Center Basin,"
Kings River Canyon, California

"Near Death Valley,"
Death Valley National Monument, California

"Kearsage Pinnacles,"
Kings River Canyon, California

"Bishop Pass,"
Kings River Canyon, California

"Boaring River, Kings Region,"
Kings River Canyon, California

"Clouds – White Pass,"
Kings River Canyon, California

"Long's Peak from Road,"
Rocky Mountain National Park, Colorado

"Evening, McDonald Lake,"
Glacier National Park, Montana

"Long's Peak,"
Rocky Mountain National Park, Colorado

"Peak above Woody Lake,"
Kings River Canyon, California

"In Glacier National Park,"
Glacier National Park, Montana

"North Dome,"
Kings River Canyon, California

"Owens Valley from Sawmill Pass,"
Kings River Canyon, California

"Heaven's Peak,"
Glacier National Park, Montana

PORTRAITS AND CLOSE-UPS

Whether because he preferred his subjects on a grand scale, or because intimate studies do not easily lend themselves to emotional interpretations, Adams did not make many portraits. He did make some studies of people, mostly for friends or on commission. His best known, of course, are those of Jimmy and Rosalynn Carter and Walter and Joan Mondale, official presidential and vice-presidential portraits taken for the National Portrait Gallery. These were quite successful, considering the pressure to succeed the first time; the only hitch came when he gently repositioned Mr. Carter's shoulders and was forcefully given to understand, by an alert secret service agent, that it is not permitted to touch the President.

Adams made many of his close-up photographs in the national parks of the U.S., as part of the Mural Project. In 1942 he visited some of the northern parks: Glacier, Yellowstone, and Mount Rainier. Yellowstone, the first and largest of our national parks, is also perhaps the most extraordinary. Among its many treasures are bubbling hot springs that smoke like a furnace and emit sulphurous gasses; and geysers, jets of steaming water spewed from underground, heated by their close proximity to the earth's molten core. Adams became enchanted with Yellowstone's geysers, "spurting plumes of white waters in sunlight against a deep blue sky." He particularly liked to photograph them when the sun was low – at dawn or at sunset – and the air took on a special clarity. In making the portrait of "Old Faithful," he was surely helped by the clock-like regularity of the geyser's eruption. Adams's "Old Faithful" is a classic example of the vibrant, deep tones and essential simplicity that characterize his best work.

Mount Rainier National Park is often obscured by clouds, even in summer, although conditions there are not as unfavorable for Adams's type of photography as in Alaska. Possibly because the weather interfered with his ability to shoot in the grandiose style he preferred, he felt that the subject matter of this park did not lend itself well to murals, so he concentrated on "photographic interpretations of nature in in-timate contact with the world." Close-up studies of small subjects such as ferns and leaves are one result of his visits to Mt. Rainier and Glacier National Parks.

These photographs are in part experiments in technique; his goal, as always, was to capture the best possible optical image of his visualization, and, through the proper use of camera, lens, filter and paper, to convey the qualities of that image to the highest degree. They are also experiments in style. The former piano student often described his work in musical terms: light was divided into tones on a scale, and a fine print could be likened to a symphony, in which the listener, or viewer, must go beyond the "broad melodic line" to explore and appreciate the "wealth of detail, forms, values, [and] the minute but vital significances" of the complete piece. Even in an intimate study of nature, Adams could see, and was able to convey, a representation of an ideal reality.

If Adams could celebrate the intimate in the imposing, if within each image of a sweeping expanse or a majestical mountain range he made his audience conscious of the significance of every detail and nuance of the photograph, he also proclaimed that even a leaf or a blade of grass could express his vision of perfection. To do this is not an easy task, but it is the task of the artist. Prolific though he was, he did not believe in the "machine gun approach" to photography; that is, shooting as much as possible in the hope that a few negatives will turn out well. An Adams print was extremely carefully crafted, from the initial visualization through the final print.

Not everybody looks at an Ansel Adams close-up and sees the inner workings of the human spirit, but then the artist does not generally pander to the crowd. When he first began teaching he tried to explain the process of visualization. One of his cardinal rules was that his students could not use his subject and composition on which to practice, but must go out and find their own. The teacher can only express a personal vision; the student can accept or reject that vision, but is always obliged to find and express the truth on his or her own terms.

"In Glacier National Park,"
Glacier National Park, Montana

"Saguaros,"
Saguaro National Monument, Arizona

"Saguaros,"
Saguaro National Monument, Arizona

"In Saguaro National Monument,"
Saguaro National Monument, Arizona

"Old Faithful Geyser,"
Yellowstone National Park, Wyoming

"Lichens,"
Glacier National Park, Montana

"In Glacier National Park,"
Glacier National Park, Montana

"Boulder Dam, 1941,"
Boulder Dam, Colorado

"Boulder Dam, 1941,"
Boulder Dam, Colorado

82

"Moraine,"
Rocky Mountain National Park, Colorado

"Rocks at Silver Gate,"
Yellowstone National Park, Wyoming

"Jupiter Terrace – Fountain Geyser Pool,"
Yellowstone National Park, Wyoming

"The Fishing Cone – Yellowstone Lake,"
Yellowstone National Park, Wyoming

"Flock in Owens Valley, 1941,"
Owens Valley, California

"Half Dome, Apple Orchard, Yosemite,"
Yosemite National Park, California

Indian Life, Past and Present

Not all of Adams's subjects are of the natural world. Buildings, people, and ancient ruins are also a part of his repertoire. People are "natural" too, of course, and yet are not thought of as natural as mountains or trees. Ancient ruins are also "natural," or at least they are made entirely of natural materials, yet they differ from mere stones or dirt in that they have been transformed by human hands into walls or adobe. If, as he implies, nature is a kind of perfection, then anything else must be something less than perfect, maybe even slightly sinister. What then are we to make of his exquisite photographs of Indians, cliff dwellings, and pueblos?

One answer is that each of his subjects must be taken on its own terms. Adams clearly thought of himself as an artist – a great craftsman, to be sure, but above all an artist. His concern was with creativity and the human spirit and ultimate truth. Although he disagreed with Minor White, a friend and fellow member of Group f/64, for his emphasis on the "introspective" and "symbolic" in photography, Adams believed that "art is a mystique and does not tolerate the dissections of cold critical analysis and aesthetic definitions."

It is easy to believe that Adams saw the Indians of the Southwest as "almost natural." Many Indians lived, and still live, in regions of incredible natural beauty, in which the activities of people were dwarfed by the sheer scope and wonder of the earth and sky. And before the Second World War many Indians of the Southwest were living in a way that had not changed a great deal in hundreds of years. Furthermore, they tended to live in harmony with their environment, so that the cliff dwellings at Mesa Verde, as well as the pueblos of the Rio Grande Valley, almost seem to be an extension of the land itself. Adams marvelled that the Navajo of the Canyon de Chelly "demonstrate that man can live with nature and sometimes enhance it," and declared that his experience of the canyon was made more "intense" by the presence of the Navajo.

Most of the subjects of Adams's Indian photographs are members of the Pueblo or Navajo tribes. One thousand years ago, what is now Mesa Verde National Park was inhabited by Anasazi Indians. The cliffs provided an excellent home: there was game in the valley, water was accessible, and the fortress was virtually unassailable. Some time in the thirteenth century, for reasons unknown, the Anasazi abandoned their homes and migrated south, there to disappear into history with barely a trace. The Pueblo, or Tewa Indians may have descended from the Anasazi. They have inhabited New Mexico's Rio Grande Valley for hundreds of years and still live there in a semi-traditional way. The Navajo, the most populous of Native Americans tribes in the U.S., inhabit areas of northwestern New Mexico and northeastern Arizona, from the Canyon de Chelly in the east to the Grand Canyon in the west.

Travel and photographic conditions were difficult in the Southwest, and Adams often wondered at the capability of earlier western photographers – traveling from site to site on the back of a mule – to attain successful results amid the heat and dust of the desert. He worked hard to achieve the lighting that would accord with his visualization of the cliff dwellings. The cliffs tend to have a yellowish color marked with dark stripes, while the recesses in which the ruins stand are shadowed and illuminated mainly by reflected light. He used a green filter to define the sunlit areas more clearly while darkening the shadows in the recesses.

Adams was influenced in his photography of the Southwest, as in other work, by early American photographers. He particularly admired the images of Timothy O'Sullivan. When Adams was sorting some photographs he made in the Canyon de Chelly, he was startled and pleased to note that he had photographed the exact scene, from the exact position, as had O'Sullivan, nearly seven decades earlier. While he found much early photography shallow, merely records of people and places, the best images he considered "glowing preceptions of the scenes, people, and the spirit of earlier days." As such he hoped to emulate them and even to push his art beyond them, into a new realm of perception and awareness.

"Canyon de Chelly,"
Canyon de Chelly, Arizona

"Church, Taos Pueblo,"
Taos Pueblo, New Mexico

"Dance, San Ildefonso Pueblo,"
San Ildefonso Pueblo, New Mexico

93

"Dance, San Ildefonso Pueblo,"
San Ildefonso Pueblo, New Mexico

"Dance, San Ildefonso Pueblo,"
San Ildefonso Pueblo, New Mexico

"Navajo Woman and Infant,"
Canyon de Chelly, Arizona

Opposite:
"Navajo Woman and Child,"
Canyon de Chelly, Arizona

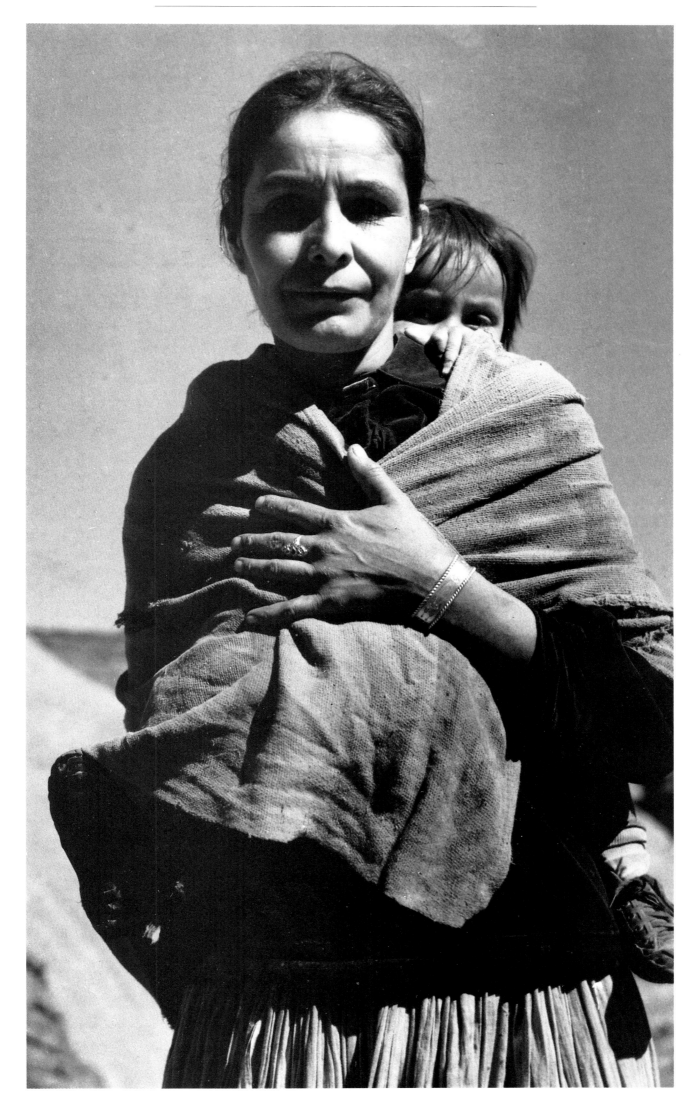

"At San Ildefonso Pueblo,"
San Ildefonso Pueblo, New Mexico

"Navajo Girl,"
Canyon de Chelly, Arizona

"Acoma Pueblo,"
Acoma Pueblo, New Mexico

"Church, Acoma Pueblo,"
Acoma Pueblo, New Mexico

"Walpi, Arizona, 1941,"
Walpi Arizona

"At Taos Pueblo,"
Taos Pueblo, New Mexico

"Corn Field, Indian Farm near Tuba City,
Arizona, in Rain, 1941,"
Tuba City, Arizona

"Interior at Ruin Cliff Palace,"
Mesa Verde National Park, Colorado

Opposite:
"Cliff Palace,"
Mesa Verde National Park, Colorado

"Cliff Palace,"
Mesa Verde National Park, Colorado

Opposite:
Untitled
Mesa Verde National Park, Colorado

"Mesa Verde National Park,"
Mesa Verde National Park, Colorado

LIST OF PHOTOGRAPHS

Photo Credits

All photographs courtesy of The National Archives except the following:
Collection of Berenice Abbott: Eugene Atget, *A Vision of Paris*: 11.
Aperture Foundation, Paul Strand, "The White Fence, Port Kent, NY, 1916," © 1971, Paul Strand Archive: 8.
Courtesy of The Art Institute of Chicago: Alfred Stieglitz, "Spring Showers," The Alfred Stieglitz Collection, 1949.849: 9.
Library of Congress: 15.
San Francisco Museum Art: Imogen Cunningham, "Magnolia Blossom, 1925," gelatin silver print, $9\frac{3}{16} \times 11\frac{5}{8}$ in., The Henry Swift Collection, Gift of Florence Alston Swift, Photo by P. Galgiani, 63.19.112: 13.

Edward Weston, "Two Shells, 1927," gelatin silver print, $9\frac{9}{16} \times 7$ in., Albert M. Bender Collection, Bequest of Albert M. Bender, Photo by Ben Blackwell, 41.2995: 17(bottom).
UCLA, University Research Library: Eadweard Muybridge, "Falls of the Yosemite from Glacier Rock," albumen print, Department of Special Collections: 7.
UPI/Bettmann Newsphotos: 10, 17(top), 18(both), 19.
Victoria and Albert Museum: Alfred Stieglitz, "The Steerage, 1907," photogravure, © Estate of Alfred Stieglitz: 12.